Contents

Easy as Pie!

There was a time, not very long ago, when building and coding computers was something only trained scientists, mathematicians, and engineers could do—or so it seemed. Today, we know that, with just a little bit of training, building and coding computers is as easy as pie!

The Raspberry Pi is an affordable microcomputer that's only about the size of a credit card. It took the world of computing by storm when it was released in early 2012. Pi's creators intended it to be used in schools to get students interested in computers and programming. In just over a year, 1 million Raspberry Pis were sold! One of the best things about Raspberry Pi is that it's affordable, making it the perfect way to experiment with and learn about computers.

Breaking the Code

Eben Upton was director of studies in computer science at the University of Cambridge's St. John's College. He noticed that fewer people were applying for a degree in computer science. In fact, most students had no idea how to code. So, he decided to make a small, simple, cheap microcomputer to encourage young people to start learning about coding. By February 2015, over 5 million Raspberry Pis had been sold!

Understanding Coding with

RASPBERRY PI™

Patricia Harris

PowerKiDS press

New York

Published in 2016 by The Rosen Publishing Group, Inc.
29 East 21st Street, New York, NY 10010

First Edition

Editor: Greg Roza
Book Design: Michael J. Flynn

Photo Credits: Cover (girl) Monkey Business Images/Shutterstock.com; cover (Raspberry Pi) JoeBreuer/Shutterstock.com; cover, pp. 1, 3–24 (coding background) Lukas Rs/Shutterstock.com; p. 5 Photofusion/Universal Images Group/Getty Images; p. 6 goodcat/Shutterstock.com; p. 7 https://commons.wikimedia.org/wiki/Category:Raspberry_Pi_by_model#/media/File:PIO_-_microSD_Adapter_for_Raspberry_Pi.jpg; p. 9 (Rasperry Pi) https://commons.wikimedia.org/wiki/Category:Raspberry_Pi_by_model#/media/File:Raspberry_Pi_running_as_an_Onion_Pi,_with_manual_focus_stacking.jpg; p. 11 Echo/Cultura/Getty Images; pp. 9 (screenshot), 12 the Raspberry Pi Foundation; p. 13 Gavin Roberts/PC Plus Magazine/Future/Getty Images; p. 15 Dj Walker-Morgan/www.flickr.com/photos/codepope/12947734983/CC BY-SA 2.0; p. 16 Rob Monk/Linux Format Magazine/Future/Getty Images; p. 17 koosen/Shutterstock.com; p. 18 parinyabinsuk/Shutterstock.com; p. 21 (teacher with students) wavebreakmedia/Shutterstock.com; p. 21 (Scratch screenshot) Scratch is developed by the Lifelong Kindergarten Group at the MIT Media Lab.

Cataloging-in-Publication Data

Names: Harris, Patricia.
Title: Understanding coding with Raspberry Pi / Patricia Harris.
Description: New York : PowerKids Press, 2016. | Series: Kids can code | Includes index.
Identifiers: ISBN 9781508144786 (pbk.) | ISBN 9781508144793 (6 pack) | ISBN 9781508144809 (library bound)
Subjects: LCSH: Raspberry Pi (Computer)–Juvenile literature. | Pocket computers–Juvenile literature. | Python (Computer program language)–Juvenile literature.
Classification: LCC QA76.8.R15 H37 2016 | DDC 004.1675–dc23

Manufactured in the United States of America

CPSIA Compliance Information: Batch #BW16PK: For Further Information contact Rosen Publishing, New York, New York at 1-800-237-9932

The Raspberry Pi may not look like much, but it can do anything a desktop or laptop computer can, such as surfing the Internet, playing games, and, of course, coding. You can also use it to make robots, cameras, games, and more!

Unboxing and Setup

A computer like Raspberry Pi is called hardware. Hardware refers to the physical parts of your computer. Software refers to the programs you run on a computer. When you first open a new Raspberry Pi, you'll find a green **circuit board**. This board has most of the parts a regular computer has, such as processing chips and **RAM**.

The Raspberry Pi microcomputer comes with ports needed to connect peripherals to it. These peripherals include a monitor, keyboard, mouse, power cord, headphones, and other **components**. Many of these peripherals connect to the Raspberry Pi using audio and video cables, as well as common **USB cords**. The Raspberry Pi also has a port for a memory card. To turn the microcomputer on, just plug it in.

You can find a lot more information about setting up and using Raspberry Pi at www.raspberrypi.org. You will also find free downloads, which you can move to the Raspberry Pi using a memory card.

Breaking the Code

The Raspberry Pi doesn't even come with a case! There are several cases you can buy for the Raspberry Pi, but many users have found interesting ways to make their own. Some users have made cases with LEGO™ blocks. Some have used a popular candy tin that happens to be the perfect size. Still others have used 3D printers! This DIY (do it yourself) way of thinking helps users have fun while learning about computers and coding.

Power Up!

All computers require software called an operating system (OS). An OS manages all the other programs and controls the computer's operations. Raspberry Pi's OS is Raspbian, which is a special **version** of the Linux OS.

When you power up the Pi, you will see the **graphical** desktop on your monitor. You will see icons for the applications, or programs, on the computer. One important icon on the desktop dropdown menu is the shutdown icon. It looks like a button with a runner on it. Use this icon when you want to turn off the Raspberry Pi. This is important because if you just unplug the microcomputer, you could damage the SD card that holds your operating system. That's not what you want to happen while learning about programming your new computer!

Breaking the Code

Linux (and Raspbian) are open-source software. That means they're free! Linux was first released in 1991. It was created by Finnish coder Linus Torvalds as an improvement over a previous open-source OS called UNIX. Torvalds created a "kernel," which is the core component of an OS. The kernel helps manage the memory of other programs and helps them open quickly.

There's one cable connected to this Raspberry Pi. It is an ethernet cable that allows the microcomputer to connect to the Internet or a network.

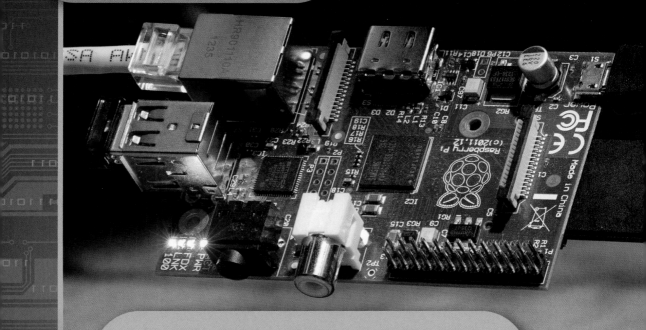

Directories and Commands

On the top bar of the opening screen is an icon that looks like a computer monitor. This is the icon for LX**Terminal** which you need to run Linux **commands**. LXTerminal lets you access the Bourne–again shell, or bash. A shell is a program that lets you enter commands from the keyboard. The bash shell gives the commands to Linux to perform your tasks.

When you open the terminal, you will be in your home **directory** and will see the prompt `pi@raspberrypi ~ $` . When coding, all your commands are entered after the "$" symbol. Linux on Raspberry Pi has all the same commands as other popular versions of Linux. Turn to page 22 to see a chart of common commands.

There are many directories in the Raspberry Pi file system. This chart shows the most common directories.

DIRECTORY	ABOUT THE DIRECTORY
/bin	Programs and commands available to all users are found here.
/dev	Contains files that are about the devices connected to your system.
/home/pi	Home directory for user called pi—that's you!
/sys	This is a special directory for devices connected to your Raspberry Pi.
/temp	A directory used by programs when they have to temporarily store files.
/usr/games	Games!
/usr/lib	A directory of files that supports programs.

Get Connected

Computers have different ways to accept input, such as a keyboard and mouse. Computers also have different ways to show output, such as a monitor and speakers. Raspberry Pi is no different, but these peripheral components don't come with the microcomputer.

The Raspberry Pi has USB ports and a port to attach it to a TV. It also has a set of general purpose input/output pins (GPIO) to make connections. These pins are wired to the computer board, but don't have special jobs like USB ports. That's why they're called general purpose. These pins allow users to do things that would be harder on a regular computer. For example, you could design a device that uses a button (input) to turn on a light (output).

general purpose input/output pins (GPIO)

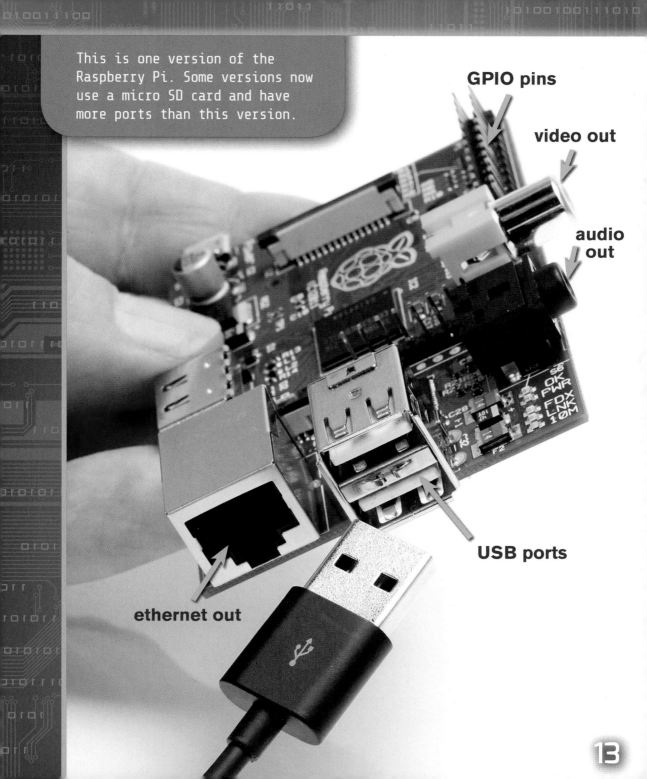

This is one version of the Raspberry Pi. Some versions now use a micro SD card and have more ports than this version.

GPIO pins

video out

audio out

USB ports

ethernet out

You can control what the GPIO pins do by using Linux commands in bash. You could connect an LED light to the GPIO pins and write the code to turn the light on and off. To program the pins on Raspberry Pi, you have to be a "superuser" and not just the "pi user." In the terminal mode, at the $ prompt, type in "sudo su." You will see that the prompt changes to `root@raspberrypi:/home/pi#` . The command "exit" takes you back.

To use the pins of the GPIO, you need to use Linux bash commands to tell the computer to send information to the pins. The command "echo 1 > value" turns the light on. "Echo 0 > value" turns the light off.

Breaking the Code

Be careful when you are at the root level in bash! This means you are a superuser. You could damage the OS because you are much more powerful at the root level than at the user level. If a superuser at the root level makes a mistake they could hurt the data on the SD card that contains your operating system. You may also have to reformat your SD card.

In this example, you use commands in bash, instead of a physical switch, to turn the light on and off.

15

Python Pi

Python, an open-source **programming language**, comes with Raspberry Pi. The microcomputer also comes with an integrated development environment (IDE) called Python and Python3. The IDE allows you to write code and see it displayed in one application. This means you don't have to write code in a text editor and then go to a terminal window to see the results.

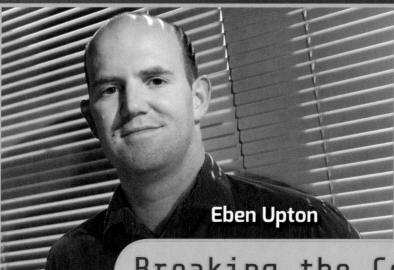

Eben Upton

Breaking the Code

When designing Raspberry Pi, Eben Upton decided that Python would be a perfect programming language for this microcomputer. "Pi" is a shortened form of the name "Python."

The IDE allows you to enter and save your Python code. It has a "Run" menu choice that lets you run your program after it's saved. To start a new program, choose "New Window" under the file menu option. After you write your program, you must save it in your home directory with the extension .py. Then you can select "Run" from the menu to see the result in the shell window.

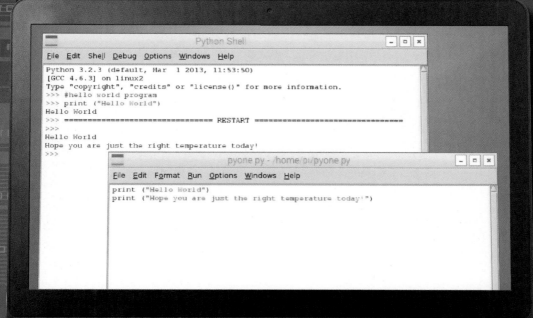

Here is an example of a simple program you can write in Python with your Raspberry Pi.

Here's a plan for a Python program: Ask the user to enter his or her name and then print the user a message with the name included. This program requires input from a user. Notice the print command at right tells users to enter their name in quotes. If they don't use quotes, the program will not get their name. Notice the line "for x in range(3):" sets up a loop. Python requires you to use an indentation of four spaces when you group work together, as when using a loop. Name your program "getname.py."

Page 19 shows a simple program in Python that includes a loop. Notice that the last line is not indented to be repeated, so it's outside the loop.

program

```
1   person = input("Enter your name in quotes:")
2   for x in range(3):
3       print "Hello" , person
4       print "Hello"
5   print "Goodbye"
```

program output

```
Enter your name in quotes: "Pat"
Hello, Pat
Hello
Hello, Pat
Hello
Hello, Pat
Hello
Goodbye
```

Breaking the Code

A loop is a set of commands grouped together so they repeat. Loops make coding easier and quicker, because you don't have to retype the code every time you want it to repeat. In Python, the "for" command is used to tell the loop when to stop. If you don't tell the loop to stop, you create an infinite loop, or one that goes on forever!

Switch to Scratch

Scratch is another programming language included on the Raspberry Pi. It's found under programming in the dropdown menu on the desktop. The program opens in its own window.

Scratch packages commands in colorful blocks that you drag and drop into an on-screen workspace. Scratch uses different types of blocks for movements, sounds, events, and more. When users put the blocks together, they create **animations**. Some blocks have curved tops and sit at the start of a program. Some blocks have indentations at the top and tabs at the bottom because they are meant to link together or stack. Some blocks have rounded or pointed ends and are variables, which give information to be included inside spaces in other blocks.

This Scratch **GUI** shows a simple program that makes a sprite (the cat) go across a stage (background). The box on the left includes all the command blocks grouped under colored tabs. The center box is where you drag the command blocks to construct your code, and your program runs in the box on the right.

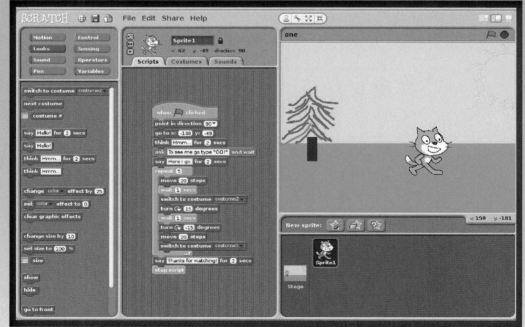

Have Fun!

By now you can see how fun and **versatile** Raspberry Pi is! You can use it to make games, flashing lights, animations, and much more. Before you can get started, it's a good idea to learn some common commands in Linux.

SOME IMPORTANT LINUX COMMANDS

COMMAND	WHAT IT DOES	EXAMPLES
cd	if ~ is used, moves you to home directory if you are not there	$ cd ~
ls	lists files in the directory	$ ls
touch	creates an empty file	$ touch new.py
mv	move files, allows you to rename files	$ mv old.py new.py
rm	removes file	$ rm
--help	gives you help on any command that comes before the --	$ rm--help
mkdir	makes a new directory	$ mkdir newdir

Glossary

animation: A movie made from a series of drawings, photographs, or computer images that creates the appearance of motion by small progressive changes in each image.

circuit board: A thin, rigid board that holds the electrical parts of a device, such as a computer.

command: A code or message that tells a computer to do something.

component: One of the parts of something.

directory: An organizational "folder" on a computer that makes finding files easier. A directory can store other directories.

graphical: Having to do with graphics, or pictures and shapes.

GUI: Pronounced GOO-ee, short for graphical user interface. A way for people to communicate with computers using images, such as windows, icons, menus, and more.

programming language: A language designed to give instructions to a computer.

RAM: Random-access memory is a chip in a computer that provides temporary memory storage. This allows programs to open and function quickly.

terminal: A computer screen or window where computer data can be viewed.

USB cord: A wire with very common connectors, used to transfer power and files from one device to another.

versatile: Able to adapt to many different functions and activities.

version: A form of something that is different from the ones that came before it.

Index

Websites

Due to the changing nature of Internet links, PowerKids Press has developed an online list of websites related to the subject of this book. This site is updated regularly. Please use this link to access the list: www.powerkidslinks.com/kcc/rasp